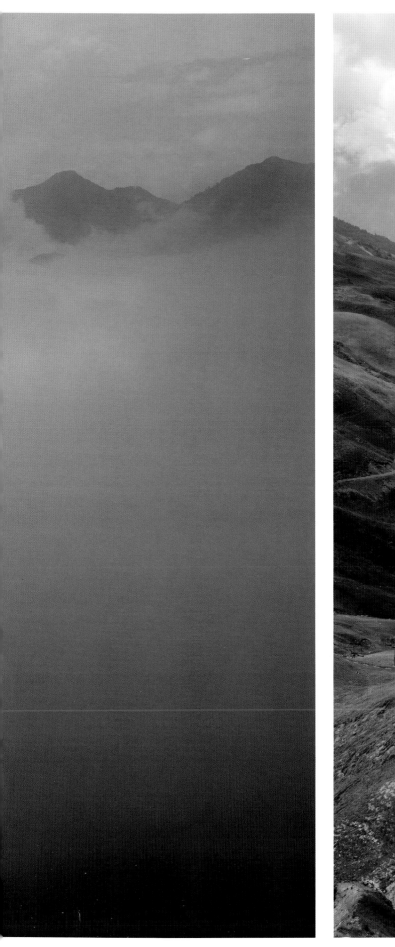

MIKE POWELL

THE GREATEST RACE

EDITED BY LEWIS BLACKWELL

ASSOCIATE EDITOR: MICHAEL HODGSON

hardie grant books
MELBOURNE · LONDON

IN ASSOCIATION WITH PQ BLACKWELL

FOREWORD

PROFESSIONAL CYCLING IS, WITHOUT DOUBT, the toughest of all sports, making the Tour de France the ultimate challenge. Just to finish the three-week trek is, for some riders, the achievement of a lifetime, while to win it is the pinnacle of any cyclist's career.

It is a sporting conflict so hard that grown men have literally limped away in tears, their morale and bodies broken beyond repair. Tragically, some have even paid with their lives, as in the cases of British rider Tom Simpson and Italian Olympic champion Fabio Casartelli – who both died in the mountains as they snaked their way towards Paris.

Since I first contracted 'Tour fever' in the 1970s, I have never missed a single day of this event that has no equal in any sport.

In the mid-80s the French wanted 'their' race to become open to the world and, after Frenchman Bernard Hinault notched his fifth win, the world obliged – and France has never won since. American Greg LeMond won in 1986, followed by Irishman Stephen Roche the year after – reports that Dubliners were jumping out of their cars to run into corner pubs, blocking traffic on a Sunday afternoon, were all true. In Great Britain viewing figures hit a record three million as Roche gave Ireland victory.

Nowadays everybody in virtually every country in the world knows of the Tour de France, and as a professional cyclist your career isn't complete without having earned a place in it at least once. From the moment a rider steps out of his hotel room he is never off-camera, and the next hotel room is his only refuge where, for a moment, the madness of the Tour can be temporarily forgotten in a restless sleep.

Cadel Evans, who became the first Australian to win The Great Race in 2011, has experienced every emotion of the Tour and is familiar with the fame and fortune that follows: recompense for the hundreds of hours spent pedalling empty lanes in the hope that one day the body will respond to the call and victory in the La Grande Boucle will become a reality.

The *Katherine Times*, the newspaper of the town where Evans was born, printed its 27 July 2011 edition in yellow – under the headline 'Cadel Our Hero' – just as the Tour's founding newspaper *L'Auto* had done when Maurice Garin won in 1903. Tour fever had reached the Northern Territory of Australia.

Since Don Kirkham and Snowy Munro became the first Australians to ride in 1914, only 42 other Aussies have ever attempted the Tour. Of these, 36 reached Paris and eight have won stages along the way, but only Phil Anderson, Stuart O'Grady, Brad McGee, Robbie McEwen and Evans have felt the intense pleasure of wearing the yellow jersey before a public of millions who fully understand the blood, sweat and tears that have gone into capturing, even briefly, *le maillot jaune*.

British riders, who only rode for the first time in 1937, have won the King of the Mountains title once – with Scot Robert Millar in 1984 – and managed to secure the green jersey for the first time in 2010 with the Isle of Man's Mark Cavendish. For Britain, 60 riders have attempted the race, with 31 finishing and nine winning stages, but the yellow jersey continues to elude.

PHIL LIGGETT,
HERTFORD, UK

"But to say that the race is the metaphor for life is to miss the point. The race is everything. It obliterates whatever isn't racing. Life is the metaphor for the race."

DONALD ANTRIM

INTRODUCTION: THE GREAT CONFUSION

THERE ARE MANY EVENTS CALLED THE TOUR DE FRANCE. THERE IS THE ONE THAT HAS a heroic winner feted around the world. There is another that features state-of-the-art machines and multiple brands vying for airtime. There are Tours of awesome endeavour and, occasionally, of boring predictability; Tours of sunshine and of rain; Tours that seem a little Belgian or Dutch, or a little Italian or Spanish, or even British, while always having the strong flavour of France. There are many more that feature local sports personalities making up the numbers in the peloton. There are others that concern the spectators, the commercial caravan of elaborate floats that precedes the race, and every town and village on the route with their own unique perspective of *their* Tour de France. And so on. Every year. For more than a century past, through the perceptions of millions of viewers each year. If our personality is as varied, or as fragmented, as the many people that we meet, as William James once suggested, then the Tour de France has as many personalities as the stars we see in the universe.

That may go some way to introducing, if not explaining, why the Tour de France is an amazing spectacle. It is an incredible cultural statement, an expression of humanity for good and bad. Every year it is a celebration and exploration of cycling; a remarkable showcase of sporting strategy and execution; and an extension and examination of French culture and beyond.

In these pages, Mike Powell has followed intimately two epic centenary tours, two tours that spanned both the good and the bad and all the various things in between. He has followed outstandingly heroic rides set against jaw-dropping scenery, gone backstage to show the preparations and procedures that typify the event, and been able to get close to the riders as they come off sapping stages. Against this, he has also had his camera on hand for the outcome of unnecessary crashes, questionable organisation or disorganisation and the general commercial babble that surrounds the event. Beyond and behind and around all this, he finds and shows France in this special moment, when as a country it ranges from displaying an unchanged and timeless geology to being a frenetic, involved participant.

This role of place in the sport cannot be underestimated and is perhaps one of the most immediate elements to note in many of the pictures. Every road race is uniquely influenced by the terrain, the weather and the random factors that day can introduce. The Tour has that multiplied across all the races in the three weeks, with different geographies and climates, from hot and windy pancake-flat coastal strips to mountain roads that can be closed off by snow even in summer.

As a deeply experienced sports photographer, Mike has been many times around the world to major events, including numerous Olympics, and into close proximity with some of the greatest athletes. He's not seduced by the glamour any more, if there is any, but is intrigued by what really makes the experience engage us. In this project his images have the added spice of cycling being the sport that is very much his most personal sporting passion. As a result, it is perhaps the quiet moments – a rider before or after a stage, the mechanics preparing the bikes, or the long, festive wait of the fans – that stand out as unusual and poignant, saying so much about the difference of this experience from the single victory snap that might usually be seen. The opportunity of the extensive photographic essay is to explore unusual narratives and ask multiple questions, not settle for offering the expected answer.

The Tour, particularly in this grand but troubling era, rewards such photographic introspection. It is too wonderful a statement of the human spirit to be wrapped up in public relations proclamations or disappear into cold statistics or be soiled in the swamp of doping allegations. Instead, as we look at these images of a luridly coloured crowd of riders on bikes, or examine the soulful, dirt- and salt-encrusted expressions of exhausted young men, or wonder at the majesty of mountains against the ant-like figures of fans and riders, we might reflect upon and enjoy the contradictions. We can accept that all the conflicting data around the Tour *is* the Tour. From its start as a ruse to sell more newspapers back in 1903, to its near collapse in a wave of disqualifications in 1904, through decade after decade of the glorious and the inglorious, this is an event that trawls into its net all manner of human experience. That is its beauty and, at times, its horror. It is not an event that can be neatly summarised. It is in so many ways a spectacle that makes us realise we are always close to finding experience, 'one great blooming, buzzing confusion', as James once described the baby's early consciousness of the world. As a sporting activity it is a long way from the comparative simplicity of a game or a match or anything that is run to a regular course. Instead this sport is more like chess being played by many players in one game, who may or may not be in alliances with each other, while the chessboard may or may not have the same number of pieces or squares as it had for the previous moves, and all the time there is an awareness that the objectives may shift and unofficial rules may be reset. There is a complex structure and bubbling potential for chaos in close proximity at all times. At the micro level it is expressed by speeding along imperfect asphalt with wheels just a few centimetres apart, disaster a small mistake away; at the macro level it is the knowledge that two hundred or so ambitious athletes are working together and against each other in numerous ways, loyalties shifting as the race progresses, as they persevere at the edge of their endurance, bound by technology, physical forces and an earpiece that links them to the thoughts of an agitated *directeur sportif*. At the still centre of all this is the mind of the rider, and it is there that races are often won and lost. Eddy Merckx, the greatest winner of Tour stages, and of all races, put it this way: 'There are too many factors you have to take into account that you have no control over … The most important factor you can keep in your own hands is yourself. I always placed the greatest emphasis on that.'

If Eddy Merckx was perhaps the greatest cyclist, his dominance of his era did not always make for the greatest Tours. Indeed, for all the greatness past of the event, there is a case to say that these are the best and the worst days for the greatest race in cycling – an event that could make a strong case to be the greatest race in the world.

Reflecting upon the best of days, the Tour de France celebrates a centenary of some of its races in 2013 and has never had a more universal following. This occasion follows closely upon centenary anniversaries of the first stages held in the Pyrenees *(1910)* and the Alps *(1911)*. The event has never been larger, from the size of the peloton – with more than 200 riders contesting the start – and up to 15 million spectators lining the roadsides, to more than 120 television stations and 400 newspapers sending their representatives to capture and relay the action around the globe. And then there are the ten million and rising unique visitors logging onto the official website, which itself is the tip of the iceberg for the online following across the Internet. This is more than one race; it is twenty-one races that lead a sport and for three weeks create a global community. This spreads outwards from the intense focus of the riders to the passions of fans crowding the roads, sometimes centimetres from the stars, a following that can easily exceed a million on several of the stages each year; and then this audience diffuses to the more silent excitement of viewers and readers taking in the daily broadcasts and newspaper columns, which cement the significance of this as a cultural landmark and an advertisement for France around the world.

Given the growing support that cycling is receiving for its association with environmental and health benefits, we might think the future could hardly be sunnier for the event. And yet true as the statistics are, a bright outlook is far from assured. The momentum of a global brand, of which the Tour de France has long been a fascinating and complex example, does not offer protection from encountering perils but acts as a target for problems.

So these can also be seen as the worst of days, where the global attention can quickly deliver massive damage to the Tour's reputation if bad news breaks. And it does. The world of professional road cycling is immensely troubled by ongoing revelations of doping. As a result, its greatest event is brought under great scrutiny and receives the greatest damage by association. Many of the winners and leading challengers of the past decade and more have either been revealed as cheats, smeared as doubtful or else had their success compromised by the banning of notable contenders.

This painful period can be interpreted in various ways. Optimists can argue that cycling is getting its house in order. They may say that it is the stringent testing regime in cycling, perhaps tougher than in any other sport, which reveals the cheats and is therefore an example of cycling actually being a cleaner sport than others. The sophisticated pharmaceutical benefits possible for the professional athletes may often remain one step ahead of the authorities, but at least cycling is more vigilant in its attempts to catch abusers than many other major sports, is one often-made argument. Meanwhile, other historians can set the troubles in a broader context: they point to the fact that doping and other forms of cheating have always been a part of the story of the Tour de France and even enrich its chapters, or at least make for entertaining anecdotes alongside sepia-toned photographs. The first winner, Maurice Garin, was disqualified from the second running of the event, along with all the other leading riders, for various offences including, reportedly, taking a train. For earlier years of the Tour (and professional cycling in general), the taking of now-banned stimulants and painkillers was routine, often permitted and even recommended by doctors – from alcohol and cocaine, to strychnine and, astonishingly, nitroglycerine (this latter 'stimulant' might be thought to give new meaning to the idea of explosive performance but is used to aid breathing and treat cardiac arrest). In more recent decades the idea of blood doping – which takes various forms but typically involves transfusing a rider with their own fresh blood that has been banked earlier – has gone from the medically advised to the outlawed. Moralists may simply say that the Tour is a manifestation of our shifting values, highlighting the tension between striving for outstanding individual achievement and our need to impose values that are for the protection of the broader community.

For the general observer, the noise of disapproval spun around the banned, illegal or otherwise controversial behaviour of cycling can distract and dismay. What are we looking at when we see a great athletic performance in the Tour? Is it sport or is it some strange display of ethically dubious sports science, pushing the body artificially to over-endure and over-achieve? How are we to feel about a sport in which one of its own ruling bodies, the Union Cycliste Internationale (UCI), secretly monitors all professional cyclists and ranks most of them with a degree of doubt over their doping practices? What are we to make of it that this story is broken by *L'Équipe*, descendant of the newspaper that started the Tour and owned by the same company that runs the event? There are many interests involved, many sides to the stories and much that detracts from the wonder of the race itself.

Victories take many forms in the Tour de France. While the main headlines go to the yellow jersey wearer as general classification winner, or to the stage winner, or to those holding jerseys green for the points winner, white for best rider under twenty-five, and polka-dot for King of the Mountains, every day brings other victories of sorts. There is even attention for the *Lanterne Rouge*, the rider in last place overall … not a sign of bad riding, more an indication of self-sacrifice, misfortune or both. Every day the most appealing story – or stories – can be less about the obvious lauded winners and more about the bravery of less heralded riders. Every cyclist in the peloton is playing their part as the race dances through the countryside, and every day many will be celebrated back on the team bus for their efforts; for giving their all as *domestiques*, or enduring a spectacular crash and then picking themselves up and riding injured to the finish, or having exhausted themselves riding at the front most of the day in a doomed break. On the road it is the adrenalin-inducing attack that fails, and yet provokes the other riders into racing better, that draws the visible respect of the crowd. Many days there is a local hero involved – raising hopes for a win or at least a sacrifice on the altar of regional pride – and for most days this is more the reality of the event for spectators than the finer minutiae of who is defending what seconds in order to have a hope for a final jersey.

It is the unpredictable mix of the individual and the collective effort, the complex ways in which suffering and glory are interchanged, and how the recipe can switch from day to day in its balance, that makes the Tour a stark reflection on existence. Stars are born, they rise or decline, occasionally careers are ended. It is so much more than a sporting event: it is a dramatisation of the tensions of life, the very cycle of life, with each day providing a fresh improvisation, testing the boundaries of what it is to strive together and separately.

When we look at the Tour, we look at ourselves, our nature – for good and bad. It is no surprise then that the Tour has triggered our fascination and affections, raising our passionate support while alarming us with the bad things it reveals about human behaviour. Don't expect ultimate resolution of this until human nature evolves.

Meanwhile, enjoy the spectacle. There is nothing else like it on earth.

"Ride your bike, ride your bike, ride your bike."

FAUSTO COPPI'S ADVICE ON WHAT IT TAKES TO BECOME A CHAMPION

"The Tour is one of the few myths of the 20th century ..."

PETER SLOTERDIJK, PHILOSOPHER

"Sometimes you're the hammer, sometimes you're the nail.
Today I was the nail."

LANCE ARMSTRONG, 2010, AFTER LOSING MINUTES AND HIS CHANCE OF WINNING AN EIGHTH AND FINAL TOUR

THE RACE

THERE IS NOTHING LIKE ONE OF THE CYCLING Grand Tours in all other sport. The grandest tour is the ultimate statement of the ultimate form of racing. In *La Grande Boucle* (the big loop, a nickname for the way the Tour encircles France) individuals and teams compete for daily, continuous and final honours. They are judged individually and yet most will sacrifice their fortunes for the team. They make alliances, agreeing to work together for a collective goal before reverting back to being competitive, and they give signals of intent that rarely mean what they seem to say. Only with hindsight can we ever be sure that a particular surge, or a seeming collapse of strength, was actually what it appeared to be. Attacks and breakaways usually come to nothing, while conversely a suffering rider may well fight back to save seconds on the day and go on to ultimate victory. In defeat we discover glory, while apparent triumph contains more than a seed of future failure. Even as they step onto the podium in Paris and have the ultimate prize of the yellow jersey placed on them, most champions are being examined for their flaws.

But that knowledge, that hindsight, comes with all the paraphernalia of live broadcast and teams of journalists feeding us their analysis. For the millions of fans on the road it is difficult, if not impossible, to know what is actually going on when the riders flash past. For them the encounter, and the pleasures, are more physical, not so much in the head as in the bodily sensation of being in a crowd or by the road or on the mountain, sharing a little of the communion with the environment that the riders are encountering. They are living the race rather than watching it.

This shared participation – no fitness or even ticketing required, just passion – is at the very heart of the appeal. As the stages roll through France, the many villages, towns and cities involved stop work and celebrate. Out come the bunting, the proudly displayed local produce, and all generations join in. The pleasure is not just for the fans who participate by the million. The combination of riders and roadside fans *are* the event for the hundreds of millions of television and online viewers. It moves it from being a simple drama to being a rich tapestry of life. The Tour has the complexity and yet assured narrative arc of a great classic of literature.

For the French philosopher Roland Barthes, the Tour was worthy of comparison with the *Odyssey* in that it combined a mass of human ordeals with testing earths limits. At the heart of the quest, indeed at the centre of the Tour's examination of France, are the mountains – the massive challenge of the Pyrenees and the Alps that tests the body beyond all normal cycling or racing comparisons. In overcoming gravity, Barthes saw the riders approaching godlike status, breaking free from the physical limits and taking control over the universe. His rich comparison strains to articulate the epic stature that hangs over a day at the Tour. It does not overstate but hints at how words can only fail to describe a cocktail that combines incredible sporting endeavour with the whole of France, and beds this on a century of tradition and mythology.

The Tour exists on the grandest of stages, the physical boundaries of France: its geology, geography and anthropology. For the fan, the race is not to an end in Paris but is a journey through many cathartic moments of tension and release, expectation and delivery. And when it is all over? Then we have the knowledge and anticipation of another year to come.

"I sleep every afternoon, go to bed at 9 p.m. I don't drink alcohol and I have no time for a girlfriend. My ambition is to participate in the Tour de France."

MATIWOS ZERAY, A PRO CYCLIST WHO REGULARLY RODE HIS NATIONAL TOUR ... THE TOUR OF ERITREA

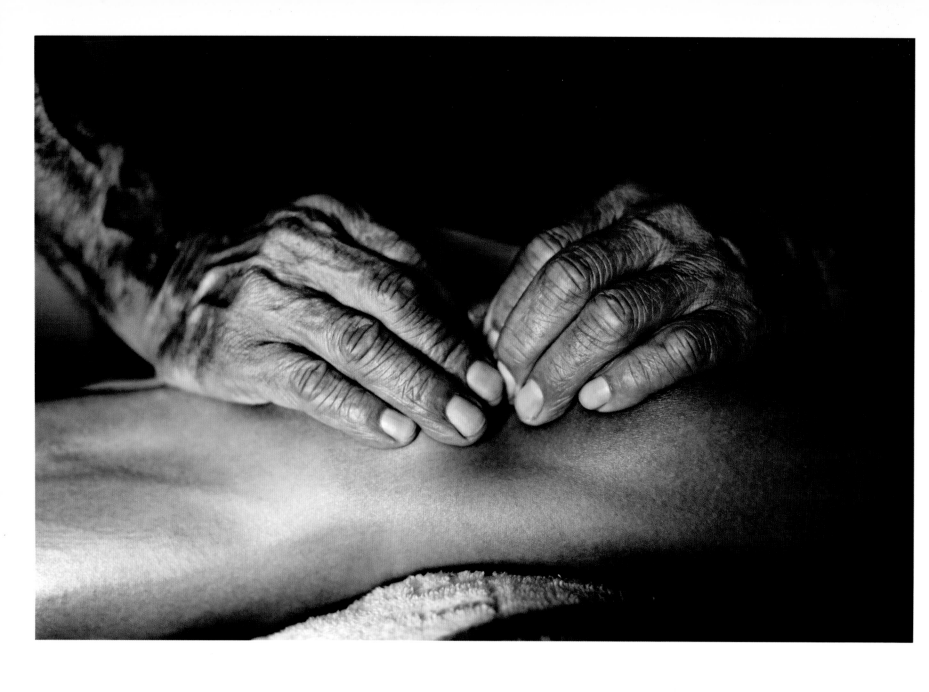

"There are no races. Only lotteries."

JACQUES ANQUETIL, FIRST TO WIN FIVE TOURS

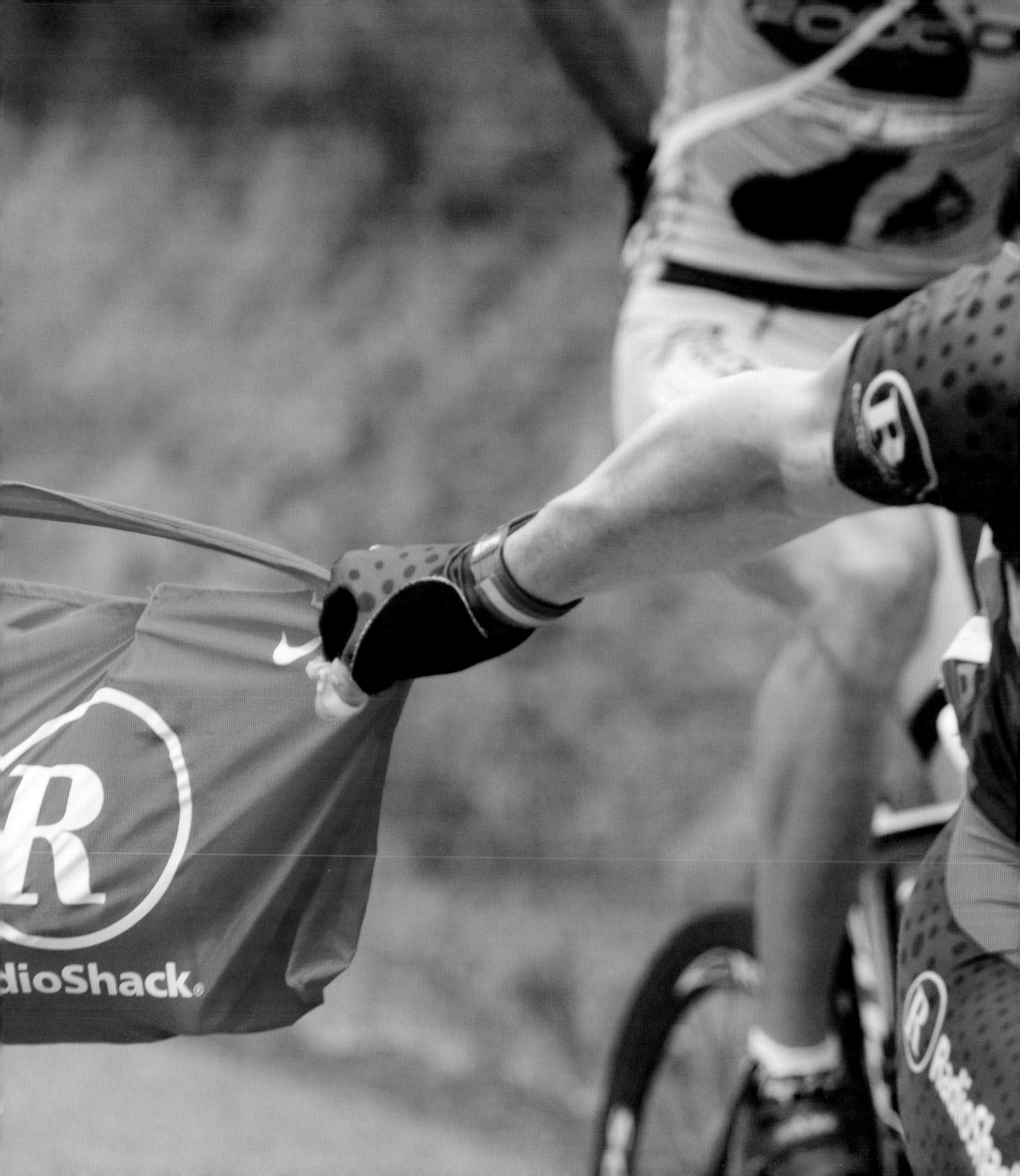
dioShack

"I did what felt like a few somersaults. I don't know where the car came from … I landed on the fence and I looked at my legs and thought, 'Is this what cycling is about?' I have the polka-dot jersey but I'm going to spend the rest day in a lot of pain."

JOHNNY HOOGERLAND, 2011, AFTER A TV CAR CRASHED INTO THE LEADING GROUP OF RIDERS ON STAGE 9

"I was hungry, I was thirsty, I was sleepy, I suffered, I cried ..."

THE BODY

IT COULD BE ARGUED THAT THE TOUR DE FRANCE has become easier over the years. The race today is typically more than 2,000 kilometres shorter than the 5,745 kilometres of 1926, the longest ever Tour, and stages average under 200 kilometres whereas the first-ever stage, in 1903, clocked 467 kilometres.

Henri Desgrange, the founding organiser, would not be amused. He saw suffering and deprivation as the basis for success. A decade before the first Tour, he wrote a training book for the aspiring racing cyclist, *La Tête et les Jambes* (Head and Legs), published in 1894. In this he included the provocative tip that an ambitious rider has no more need of a woman than an unwashed pair of socks. In developing the race he set out to test the human body to its limits – and beyond. 'The ideal Tour would be a Tour where only a single rider would finish the race,' he said. For many years he was opposed to permitting Tour riders to tackle the event on anything other than a fixed-gear machine, as if multiple gear ratios were a sign of physical degeneracy.

Maurice Garin, after winning the first Tour, described the experience as being one where: 'I was hungry, I was thirsty, I was sleepy, I suffered, I cried…' The rules required him to win without team-mates or mechanical back-up. It may seem that the modern champion has it easy. Protected by his *domestiques*, supported by the team car with a spare bike or two, he is kept in drinks and food until the moment when he needs to make or repel an attack. When the ride is over, rapid and careful refuelling is on hand in the team bus, with expert massaging delivered at the next hotel.

Had Desgrange been around for the first rest day in 2011, he would have been shocked by how riders prepared. Cadel Evans was spending the afternoon in his hotel room with his wife, Chiara Passerini, and dog, Molly. He went on to win the event. Meanwhile, Mark Cavendish had the support of his buxom glamour-model girlfriend, Peta Todd. 'No Wonder He Won!' lasciviously dribbled the British *Daily Mail* newspaper later as Cavendish took the green jersey for the overall points victory.

The Tour has not become a softer challenge, but has evolved into being a very different one from the first events. The geography of the ride keeps exploring into the full potential of France. Indeed, in 2011 the highest-ever stage finish was achieved, 2,645 metres atop the Col du Galibier, marking the hundredth anniversary of the Alps in the Tour, with a record altitude difference for the stage of 2,444 metres. By shortening stages (around a six-hour maximum now compares to early marathons that extended through the night and across two days) and allowing riders to aid each other and work as a team, the focus has moved to searching examinations of different attributes. The Tour organisers tune the event to test the range of the road-cyclist physique: short and longer time trials, rolling stages ending on a sharp climb, long flat stages ending in a sprint, or massively mountainous days ending atop the toughest climbs. At the end of a long stage it is estimated that Cavendish can still pump out 1,600 watts of power to take the sprint, while during the mountainous stage a rider will burn 6,000–8,000 calories per day, depending on their size. As Evans almost closed the gap between himself and Andy Schleck on that Galibier finish, he was able to inhale and exhale at about double the capacity of the average man. These statistics and others place the pro peloton riders as athletes at the evolutionary edge of physical development.

"It never gets easier, you just go faster."

GREG LEMOND, THREE-TIME WINNER, INCLUDING VICTORY BY JUST EIGHT SECONDS IN 1989

"You are assassins, yes, assassins!"

OCTAVE LAPIZE, 1910, ON THE AUBISQUE,
THE FIRST TOUR TO PASS THROUGH THE PYRENEES

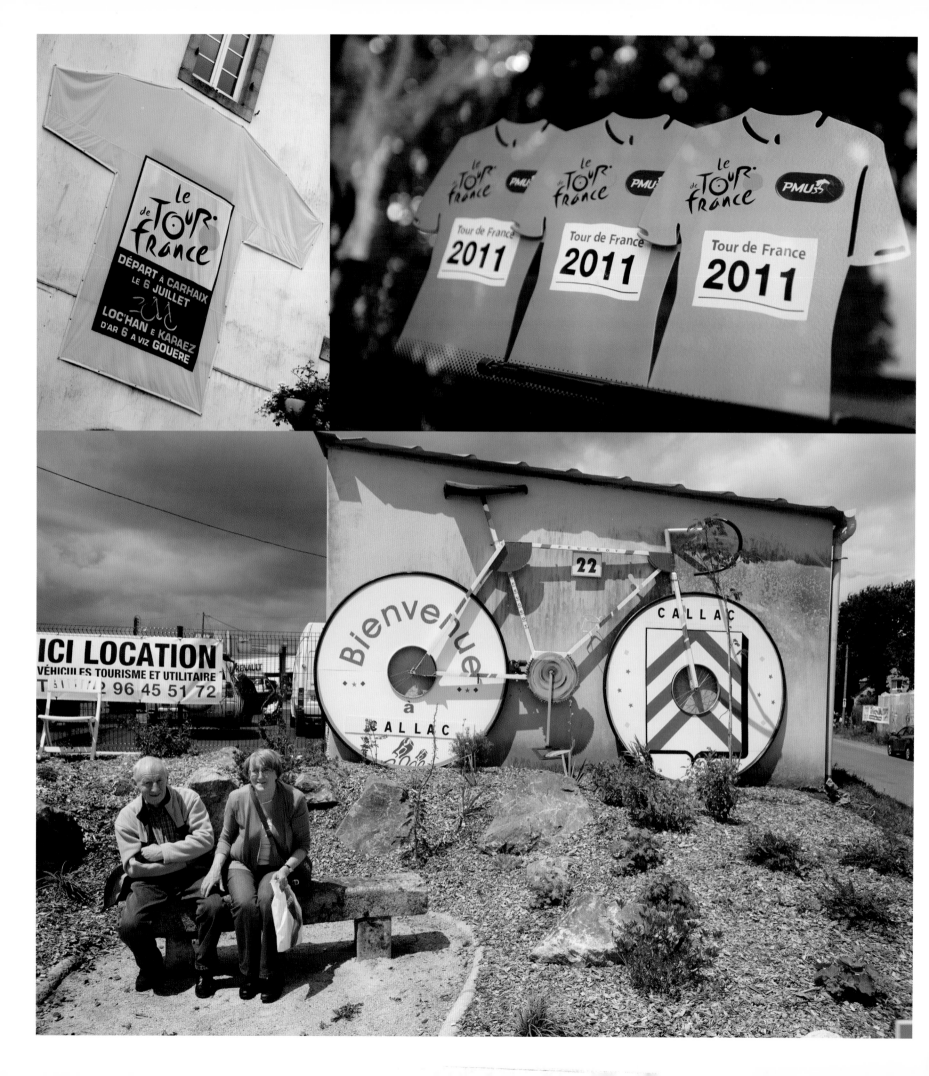

SOMMET
1km

"If I had attacked one more time I would have dropped myself."

ANDY SCHLECK, DURING THE 2010 TOUR, AS HE FOUGHT IN VAIN TO REGAIN THE LEAD

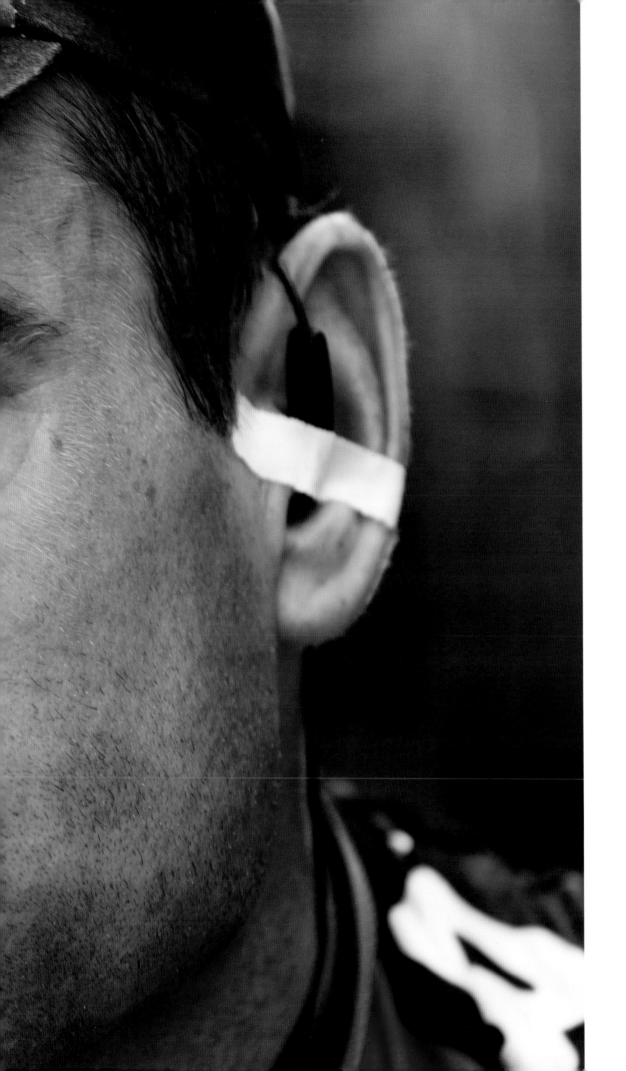

THE SPIRIT

STATISTICS TELL US THE TOUR IS A PHYSICAL challenge where only the fittest can survive. Reel out the numbers and the references concerning the distance covered and the time taken, note the metres climbed, the extremes of weather, and don't forget the strength and depth of the competition. It makes a daunting list of reasons why only the most remarkable cyclists can endure the three weeks, let alone thrive in July. However, this does not make it the greatest race. The other Grand Tours – Italy's Giro, Spain's Vuelta – offer much of the same and often tougher climbs, hotter days and longer stages. What makes the Tour the greatest race is that it is … the Tour de France.

The Tour is its own belief system. It is a religion or a megabrand, depending on your taste. Because it has the heritage of being the greatest race, because it never fails to deliver grand actions on a grand stage, it remains ahead of all others. Great as the Giro may be, it is not the Tour. If the fans, the media and commercial interests conspire to say the Tour is the most important, then it is.

This is not a con, and it is only an illusion in the sense that so many of the things we cherish most are in fact illusions. This is the reality determined by an agreement of many people and enterprises that, year after year, ensures the Tour is the focal point of the cycling year. At the centre of this agreement, beyond the many millions watching and the many millions of euros, dollars and the rest piled behind vested interests, are just two hundred or so individuals – the riders. And on them rests the whole structure of belief: the Tour is the greatest race because they provide the credibility to make it so. It is because they believe that all others can believe. Whether sprinters, climbers, *rouleurs* or *puncheurs*, team

leaders or junior *domestique*s – whatever kind of rider, they want to be at the Tour. It tells them they are in the first rank of their sport. To take part is an achievement, to be part of a team that has winners is a thrill, and to be a stage winner, a wearer of one of the jerseys, or even an overall contender for the yellow jersey – this is the essence of being alive for the professional road cyclist.

And why do they believe? The cynic may say that they have grown up with that belief system, working their way through the cycling ranks until they achieve the status of being a Tour rider: they have been brought up in the faith and will naturally support and defend it. The Tour is where it is in status because history gives it momentum and inertia prevents easy change to alternatives.

But there is more, so much more. To see riders commit to the race and to hear them describe their experience is to realise that for them it approaches a spiritual experience, a journey deep within themselves that engages everything that defines them. They often do things that are not a repetition of what they achieved in training but are expressions of who they are. Take Thomas Voeckler in the 2011 race – once he was in the yellow jersey he was carrying the hopes of France. He was expressing the showmanship and bravado that is both his character and what he felt the fans needed to see. Both France and Voeckler knew he was almost certainly going to lose the lead but it was the courage with which he held it, and finally conceded the position, that expressed the spirit we all sought. This was so much more than athleticism, this was grand theatre, and France was a stage on which we saw performed a morality tale.

For that spirit, that spiritual life that even the most secular of us can savour, we worship at the altar of the Tour.

"Cycling isn't a game, it's a sport. Tough, hard and unpitying, and it requires great sacrifices. One plays football, or tennis, or hockey. One doesn't play at cycling."

JEAN DE GRIBALDY, MANAGER OF SEAN KELLY, FOUR-TIME GREEN JERSEY

"To win, sprinters must have everything: physical condition, confidence, luck, aggression and committed team support. An elusive combination, attainable but not sustainable."

DAVID WALSH

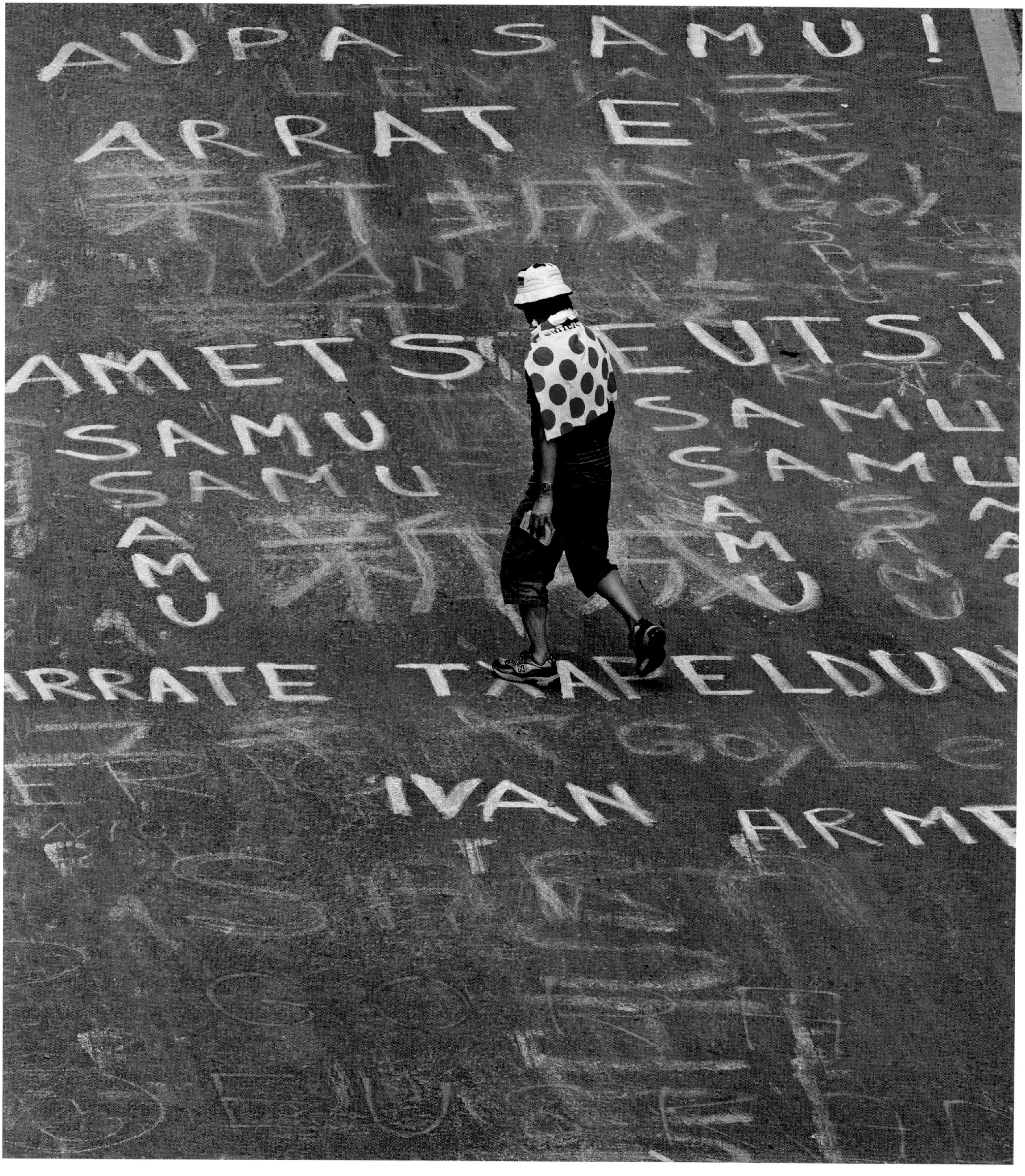
AUPA SAMU!
ARRATE
SAMU
SAMU
SAMU
SAMU
IVAN

"Contador just gained a great chance to win,
but he lost the chance to win greatly."

CERVÉLO TEAM OWNER GERARD VROOMEN, 2010,
ON CONTADOR ATTACKING WHEN SCHLECK DROPPED HIS CHAIN

"Today represents a brand new entry into my top five worst-ever days on a bike …
I spent 180 kilometres by myself convinced I was going to abandon or be eliminated."

DAVID MILLAR, 2010,
AFTER FINISHING LAST ON STAGE 9,
42 MINUTES BEHIND THE WINNER

"From Paris to the blue waves of the Mediterranean, from Marseille to Bordeaux, passing along the roseate and dreaming roads, sleeping under the sun, across the calm of the fields of the Vendée, following the Loire, which flows on still and silent, our men are going to race madly, unflaggingly."

HENRI DESGRANGE,
FOUNDER AND PROMOTER OF THE TOUR

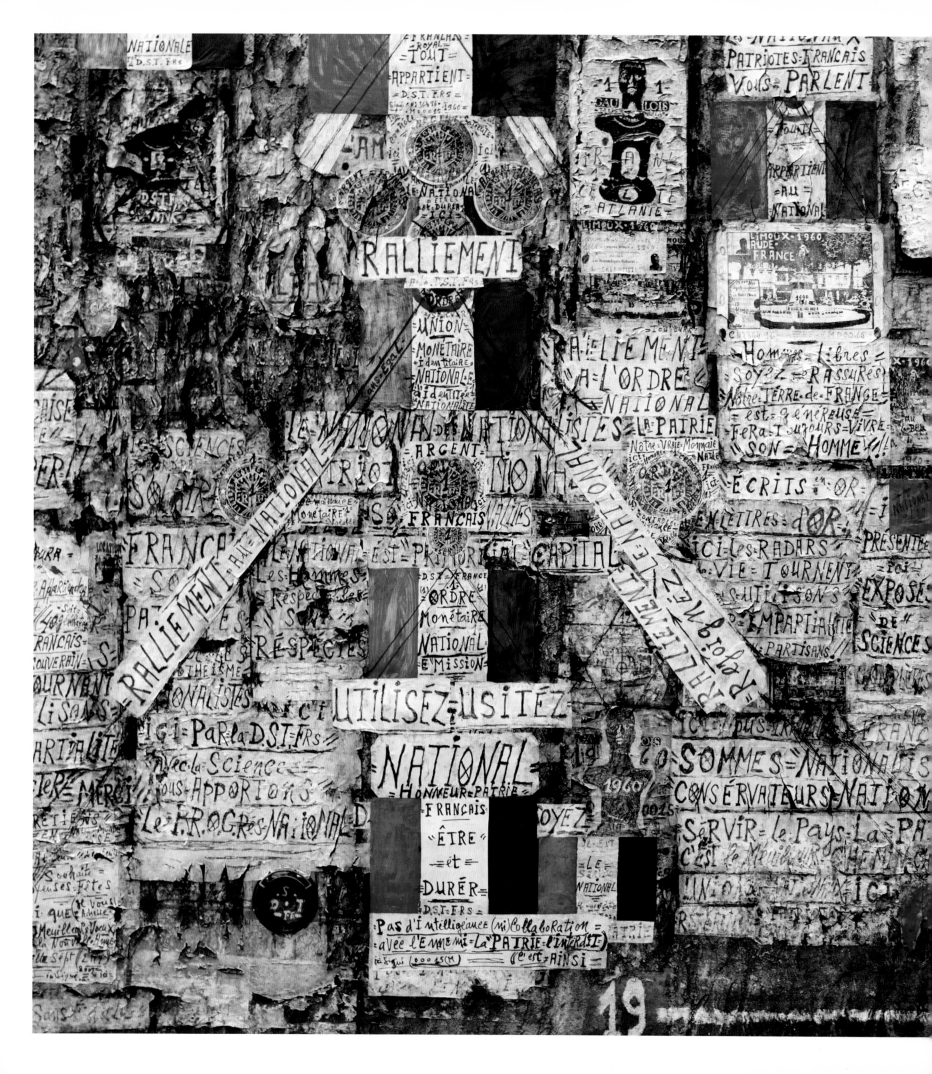

"The ideal Tour would be a Tour where only a single rider would manage to finish the race."

HENRI DESGRANGE,
FOUNDER AND PROMOTER
OF THE TOUR

Fans wait on the slopes of the Col de la Madeleine, *Stage 9, 13 July 2010.*

CANON EOS 1D MKIV, 70-200M, 640SEC @ F8, F2.8L IS USM.

Looking west from the Col du Tourmalet, 2010 and 2011 Tours.

CANON EOS 5D MKII, 50MM, 1250/500SEC @ F9, ISO 100/F1.2L USM.

Fans enjoy summer on the *pavé* (cobblestone) section at Haveluy, *Stage 3, 6 July 2010.*

CANON EOS 5D MKII, 50MM, 125SEC @ F16/ 500SEC @ F8, ISO 100.

Fans waiting patiently on the Morzine-Avoriaz, *Stage 8, 11 July 2010.*

CANON EOS 1D MKIV, CANON 16-35MM, 1250SEC @ F5, ISO 200.

Flags on the slopes of the Col du Noyer, *Stage 10, 14 July 2010.*

CANON EOS 5D MKII, 50MM, 500SEC @ F8, F1.2 ISO 100.

Fans waiting on the slopes of the Col d'Aubisque, *Stage 13, 15 July 2011.*

CANON EOS 5D MKII, CANON EF 50MM, 2500SEC @ F2, ISO 100/F1.2L USM.

Fans wait on the high, cold pass of the Col du Tourmalet, *Stage 12, 14 July 2011.*

CANON EOS 1D MKIV, 70-200MM, 800SEC @ F3.5, F2.8L IS USM.

The aftermath of a pre-Tour lunch, *Stage 7, 10 July 2010.*

CANON EOS 5D MKII, CANON EF 16-35MM, F2.8 II USM, 400SEC @ F5.6, ISO 200.

Fans, *Stages 4, 9 & 6, July 2010.*

CANON EOS 1D MKIV, CANON EF 50MM, F1.2L USM, 640SEC @ F5.6, ISO 100.

Young and old enjoying the *départ* in Pinerolo, Italy, *Stage 18, 18 July 2011.*

CANON EOS 5D MKII, CANON EF 50MM, F1.2L USM, 8000SEC @ F2, ISO 100.

Tournus, *Stage 7, 10 July 2010;* Saint-Paul-Trois-Châteaux, *Stage 16, 19 July 2011.*

CANON EOS 5D MKII, CANON EF 16-35MM, F2.8L II USM, 640SEC @ F9/125SEC @ F13, ISO 200.

Rubén Pérez Moreno: Bourg-de-Péage and Col du Tourmalet, *Stages 12 & 16, July 2010.*

CANON EOS 5D MKII, CANON EF 50MM, F1.2L USM, 400SEC @ F2.8/2000SEC @ F2.8, ISO 200.

Robert Gesink, Tournus; Geraint Thomas, Paris, *Stages 7 & 20, July 2011.*

CANON EOS 1D MKIV, EF 70-200/500MM, F2.8 IS II/F4L USM, 500SEC @ F7. 1/1250SEC @ F5.6, ISO 200.

Peloton rides up the Col du Noyer, *Stage 10, 14 July 2010.*

CANON EOS 1D MKIV, CANON EF 16-35MM, F2.8 II USM, 500SEC @ F7, ISO 200.

Peloton crosses the Passage du Gois for the start, *Stage 1, 2 July 2011.*

CANON EOS 1D MKIV, CANON EF 70-200MM, F2.8 IS II USM, 800SEC @ F11, ISO 200.

Stormy sky over the peloton and the Mont-Saint-Michel, *Stage 6, 7 July 2011.*

CANON EOS 5D MKII, CANON EF 50MM, F1.2L USM, 800SEC @ F8, ISO 200.

Peloton rides through farmland on the way to Reims, *Stage 4, 7 July, 2010.*

CANON EOS 5D MKI, 35MM, F1.4L USM, 800SEC @ F8, ISO 100.

Peloton heads south away from Le Mans, *Stage 7, 8 July 2011.*

CANON EOS 1D MKIV, CANON EF 70-200MM, F2.8 IS II USM, 1250SEC @ F7, ISO 200.

Riding flat-out, sunflower fields, *Stage 15, 19 July 2010.*

CANON EOS 1D MKI, CANON EF 70-200MM, F2.8 IS II USM, 13SEC @ F32, ISO 100.

Different villages, different receptions.

CANON EOS 1D MKIV, CANON EF 70-200/ 500MM, F2.8 IS II USM/F4L USM, 1000SEC @ F8/1600SEC @ F6.3, ISO 200.

The hard edge of *pavé*, near Arenberg, *Stage 3, 6 July 2010.* CANON EOS 5D MKII, CANON EF 50MM, F1.2L USM, 640SEC @ F7.1, ISO 100.

Fans wait and Armstrong's last ride up the *pavé*, near Arenberg, *Stage 3, 6 July 2010.* CANON EOS 5D MKII, CANON EF 16-35MM, F2.8 II USM, 1250SEC @ F5 ISO 100/800SEC @ F6.3, ISO 200.

The playing field, Cholet, *Stage 2 team time trial, 3 July 2011.* CANON EOS 1D MKIV, CANON EF 500MM, F4L USM, 1600SEC @ F6.3, ISO 200.

Team FDJ pushes through the heat haze, Cholet, *Stage 2 team time trial, 3 July 2011.* CANON EOS 1D MKIV, CANON EF 500MM, F4L USM, 1000SEC @ F6.3, ISO 250.

Dave Zabriskie leads the Garmin-Cervélo team to victory, Cholet, *Stage 2 team time trial, 3 July 2011.* CANON EOS 1D MKIV, CANON EF 500MM, F4L USM, 1000SEC @ F6.3, ISO 250.

Waiting for the Tour, Figeac, *Stage 10, 12 July 2011.* CANON EOS 5D MKII, CANON EF 16-35/50MM, F2.8 II/F1.2L USM, 320SEC @ F5.6/1250SEC @ F2, ISO 100.

Lorient, *Stage 4, 5 July 2011.* CANON EOS 5D MKII, CANON EF 50MM, F1.2L USM, 500/1000SEC @ F2, ISO 100.

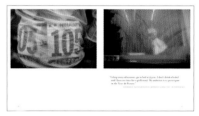

Covering up and hiding from the rain, Lorient, *Stage 4, 5 July 2011.* CANON EOS 5D MKII, CANON EF 50MM, F1.2L USM, 1600SEC/500SEC @ F2, ISO 100.

Team HTC drags the peloton in pursuit of the break, *Stage 11, 13 July 2011.* CANON EOS 5D MKII, CANON EF 50MM/ 70-200MM, F1.2L USM/F2.8 IS II USM, 3200SEC @ F2/400SEC @ F3.5, ISO 250/320.

Peloton, *Stage 11, 13 July 2011.* CANON EOS 1D MKIV, CANON EF 70-200MM, F2.8 IS II USM, 2000SEC @ F2.8, ISO 640.

Thor Hushovd (L), Redon, *Stage 3, 4 July 2011.* CANON EOS 1D MKIV, CANON EF 500/70-200MM, F4L USM/F2.8 IS II USM, 1000SEC @ F5.6/ 400SEC @ F4.5, ISO 200.

Serge Pauwels (R) and Team Sky, *Stage 13, 17 July 2010.* CANON EOS 5D MKII, CANON EF 50MM, F1.2L USM, 125SEC @ F2, ISO 800.

Bike maintenance. CANON EOS 1D MKIV, CANON EF 50MM, F1.2L USM, 400SEC @ F2.8, ISO 800.

Rag Murugayan and Diego Costa, Team Sky mechanics prepping bikes, *12 July 2010.* CANON EOS 1D MKIV, CANON EF 50MM, F1.2L USM, 250SEC @ F1.8, ISO 200.

Parts and preparation, *rest day, 12 July 2010.* CANON EOS 1D MKIV, CANON EF 50MM, F1.2L USM, 250SEC @ F1.8, ISO 200.

Station des Rousses–Morzine-Avoriaz (L), Rodez–Revel, *Stages 8 & 13, July 2010.* CANON EOS 5D MKI, CANON EF 16-35/50MM, F2.8 II USM/ F1.2L USM, 500SEC @ F14/250SEC @ F2, ISO 100.

George Hincapie, Galabier, *Stage 18, 21 July 2011.* CANON EOS 1D MKI, CANON EF 50MM, F1.2L USM, 125SEC @ F2, ISO 100.

Pau–Col du Tourmalet, *Stage 16, 22 July 2010.* CANON EOS 1D MKIV, CANON EF 70-200MM, F2.8 IS II USM, 250SEC @ F3.5, ISO400.

Details of the steeds, France, *2010/2011.*

Riders prepare in Lourdes, *Stage 13, 15 July 2011.* CANON EOS 5D MKII, CANON EF 50MM, F1.2L USM, 1250SEC @ F2, ISO 100.

The *soigneurs* (assistants) wait to feed their hungry riders, France, *2010/2011.*

Domestiques (literally servants) Arthur Vichot and Grisha Niermann make sure their teammates are fed and watered, France, *2010/2011.*

Injured riders; Johnny Hoogerland (R) climbing the Alpe d'Huez, *Stage 19, 22 July 2011.*

CANON EOS 1D MKIV, CANON EF 70–200MM, F2.8 IS II USM, 640SEC @ F6.3, ISO 160.

Riders' faces, France, *2010/2011;* Matti Bresche, Bourg-de-Péage–Mende, *Stage 12, 16 July 2010.*

CANON EOS 1D MKIV, CANON EF 70–200MM, F2.8 IS II USM, 1000SEC @ F2.8, ISO 400.

A tough finish up the Mûr-de-Bretagne, Arthur Vichot (R), *Stage 4, 5 July 2011.*

CANON EOS 1D MKIV, CANON EF 50MM, F1.2L USM, 2500 @ F2, ISO 100.

Geraint Thomas after a hard finish up the Mûr-de-Bretagne, *Stage 4, 5 July 2011.*

CANON EOS 1D MKIV, CANON EF 50MM, F1.2L USM, 2500 @ F2, ISO 100.

The *hors catégorie* (literally beyond categorising) climb, Port de Pailhères, *Stage 14, 18 July 2010.*

CANON EOS 1D MKIV, CANON EF 50MM, F1.2L USM, 5000 @ F2, ISO 100.

Stage-winner Christophe Riblon (L) and Anthony Charteau, Port de Pailhères, *Stage 14, 18 July 2010.*

CANON EOS 1D MKIV, CANON EF 50MM, F1.2L USM, 5000 @ F2, ISO 100.

Sammy Sanchez, Luz-Ardiden, *Stage 12, 14 July 2011;* Col de la Croix de la Serra, *Stage 7, 10 July 2010.*

CANON EOS 5D MKII, CANON EF 16–35MM, F2.8 II USM, 800SEC @ F6.3, ISO 200.

Ivan Velasco, Col du Tourmalet, *Stage 16, 20 July 2010.*

CANON EOS 5D MKII, CANON EF 16–35MM, F2.8 II USM, 500SEC @ F8, ISO 100.

Contador, Schleck, Costa and Riblon, Col du Galibier, *Stage 19, 22 July 2011.*

CANON EOS 5D MKII, CANON EF 16–35MM, F2.8 II USM, 640SEC @ F5.6, ISO 100.

Peloton ascends the *hors catégorie* Col Agnel, Italy–France, *Stage 18, 21 July 2011.*

CANON EOS 5D MKII, CANON EF 16–35MM, F2.8 II USM, 500SEC @ F9, ISO 200.

Col du Galibier, *Stage 19, 22 July 2011.*

CANON EOS 1D MKIV, CANON EF 16–35MM, F2.8 II USM, 60SEC @ F2.8, ISO 100.

British fans enjoy a day in the Alps, *Stage 14, 15 July 2011.*

CANON EOS 5D MKII, CANON EF 16–35MM, F2.8 II USM, 250SEC @ F11, ISO 100.

The *caravane publicitaire* (publicity caravan) winds its way through the Alps, *2010.*

The *caravane publicitaire* winds its way through the Alps, France, *2010/2011.*

Citroën *deux-chevaux* (two-horse) club, *Stage 7, 8 July 2011.*

CANON EOS 5D MKII, CANON EF 50MM, F1.2L USM, 400SEC @ F8, ISO 100.

Campsite in the Pyrénées, *Stage 14, 15 July 2011.*

CANON EOS 5D MKII, CANON EF 16–35MM, F2.8 II USM, 250SEC @ F11, ISO 100.

A cycling enthusiast's roadside display, *Stage 13, 15 July 2011.*

CANON EOS 1D MKIV, CANON EF 16–35MM, F2.8 II USM, 250SEC @ F10, ISO 100.

Jerseys, bikes and flowers adorn the Tour's stages, France, *2010/2011.*

The King of the Mountain *maillot à pois rouges* (polka-dot jersey), France, *2010/2011*.
CANON EOS 1D MKIV, CANON EF 70-200MM, F2.8 IS II USM, 25SEC @ F10, ISO 100.

The King of the Mountain *maillot à pois rouges* (polka-dot jersey), France, *2010/2011*.
CANON EOS 1D MKIV, CANON EF 70-200MM, F2.8 IS II USM, 25SEC @ F10, ISO 100.

The podium, kisses, flowers and plushy lions, France, *2010/2011*.

Andy Schleck, Bourg-de-Péage, *Stage 12, 16 July 2010*.
CANON EOS 1D MKIV, CANON EF 70-200MM, F2.8 IS II USM, 320SEC @ F5.6, ISO 200.

Cadel Evans, Galibier, *Stage 18, 21 July 2011*.
CANON EOS 1D MKIV, CANON EF 70-200MM, F2.8 IS II USM, 40SEC @ F4, ISO 100.

Jens Voight and Christian Vande Velde, France, *2011*.
CANON EOS 5D MKII, CANON EF 50MM, F1.2L USM, 2000SEC @ F2, ISO 200.

Tom Danielson, Grenoble, *Stage 20 individual time trial, 23 July 2011*.
CANON EOS 5D MKII, CANON EF 50MM, F1.2L USM, 2000SEC @ F2, ISO 200.

The speed of the road, France, *2011*.

The last kilometre: Alberto Contador (L) sprints to close the gap, Mark Cavendish sprints to win, *2011*.
CANON EOS 1D MKIV, CANON EF 500MM, F2.8L IS USM, 2000SEC F5.6, ISO 250.

Peloton approaches the finish line, Mark Cavendish will win the sprint, Châteauroux, *Stage 7, 8 July 2011*.
CANON EOS 1D MKIV, CANON EF 500MM, F4L IS USM, 1250SEC F4.5, ISO 400.

André Greipel wins, Carmaux, *Stage 10, 12 July 2011*.
CANON EOS 1D MKIV, CANON EF 70-200MM, F2.8 IS II USM, 1250SEC @ F4, ISO 320.

Philippe Gilbert celebrates his win, Mont des Alouettes, Les Herbiers, *Stage 1, 2 July 2011*.
CANON EOS 1D MKIV, CANON EF 500MM, F4L IS USM, 1000SEC @ F5.6, ISO 400.

Mark Cavendish celebrates his seventeenth stage-victory, Châteauroux, *Stage 7, 8 July 2011*.
CANON EOS 5D MKII, CANON EF 50MM, F1.2L USM, 1600SEC @ F2, ISO 100.

Looking down the valley to La Grave, between the Col du Galibier and Alpe d'Huez.
CANON EOS 1D MKIV, CANON EF 70-200MM, F2.8 IS II USM, 500SEC @ F9, ISO 100.

Campers settle in on the Port de Balès, Pyrénées, *Stage 15, 19 July 2010*.
CANON EOS 5D MKII, CANON EF 16-35MM, F2.8 II USM, 500SEC @ F9, ISO 100.

Campers on the slopes of the Col du Tourmalet, Pyrénées, *19 July 2010*.
CANON EOS 5D MKII, CANON EF 16-35MM, F2.8 II USM, 200SEC @ F5.6, ISO 200.

Fans waiting in the mist on the Col du Tourmalet, Pyrénées, *Stage 16, 22 July 2010*.

Two views of the same road on the Col du Tourmalet, Pyrénées, *Stage 15, 20 July 2010*.
CANON EOS 1D MKIV, CANON EF 70-200MM, F2.8 IS II USM, 800SEC F6.3, ISO 200.

Col du Tourmalet, Pyrénées, *Stage 15, 20 July 2010*.
CANON EOS 5D MKII, CANON EF 16-35MM, F2.8 II USM, 800SEC @ F8, ISO 200.

Alpe d'Huez, Plateau de Beille; Jelle Vanendert, *Stage 14, 15 July 2011*.
CANON EOS 1D MKIV, CANON EF 70-200MM, F2.8 IS II USM.

Fans on the slopes of the Col de la Madeleine, *Stage 9, 13 July 2010.*

CANON EOS 1D MKIV, CANON EF 16-35MM, F2.8 II USM, 1250SEC @ F5.6, ISO 200.

The mountains: a chance to break away; Contador and Schleck, 1 kilometre from the finish on the Col du Tourmalet, Pyrénées, *Stage 16, 22 July 2010.*

Art imitating life: Anthony Charteau (R) wears the polka-dot jersey, Col du Tourmalet, *Stage 16, 22 July 2010.*

David Millar, Col du Tourmalet, *Stage 16, 22 July 2010.*

CANON EOS 5D MKII, CANON EF 50MM, F1.2L USM, 640SEC @ F2.8, ISO 100.

Route des Alpes, Col d'Izoard, *Stage 18, 20 July 2011.*

CANON EOS 5D MKII, CANON EF 50MM, F1.2L USM, 8000SEC @ F2, ISO 100.

Col Agnel, *20 July 2011.*

CANON EOS 5D MKII, CANON EF 50MM, F1.2L USM, 8000SEC @ F2, ISO 100.

Looking back into France from Italy and the Col Agnel, *20 July 2011.*

CANON EOS 5D MKII, CANON EF 50MM, F1.2L USM, 8000SEC @ F2, ISO 100.

Wall statement, Pau, *Stage 13, 15 July 2011.*

CANON EOS 5D MKII, CANON EF 50MM, F1.2L USM, 8000SEC @ F2, ISO 100.

Alberto Contador and Cadel Evans, Bordeaux–Pauillac, *Stage 19 time trial, 24 July 2010.*

Peloton runs across the cobbles of the Place de la Concorde, Paris, *Stage 20, 25 July 2010.*

CANON EOS 5D MKII, CANON EF 50MM, F1.2L USM, 100SEC @ F13, ISO 100.

Peloton, Champs-Élysées, Paris, *Stage 20, 25 July 2010.*

CANON EOS 5D MKII, CANON EF 50MM, F1.2L USM, 100SEC @ F13, ISO 100.

Peloton, Champs-Élysées, Paris, *Stage 21, 24 July 2011.*

CANON EOS 5D MKII, CANON EF 16-35MM, F2.8 II USM, 60SEC @ F16, ISO 100.

Mark Cavendish with 200 metres to go to win, Champs-Élysées, *Stage 20, 25 July 2010.*

CANON EOS 5D MKII, CANON EF 50MM, F1.2L USM, 160SEC @ F11, ISO 200.

Mark Cavendish celebrates victory on the Champs-Élysées and the green jersey, *Stage 21, 24 July* 2011.

CANON EOS 5D MKII, CANON EF 50MM, F1.2L USM, 640SEC @ F2, ISO 100.

Tour winner, Cadel Evans and the Schleck brothers, Paris, *Stage 21, 24 July 2011.*

CANON EOS 1D MKIV, CANON EF 500MM, F4L IS USM, 1000SEC @ F4.5, ISO 200.

Team award, *25 July 2010;* End of an era: Lance Armstrong (R) on his final Tour.

CANON EOS 1D MKIV, CANON 70-200MM, F2.8L IS USM, 1000SEC @ F4.5, ISO 200.

Mark Cavendish rides the Champs-Élysées on the team parade, *Stage 20, 25 July 2010.*

CANON EOS 5D MKII, CANON EF 50MM, F1.2L USM, 8000SEC @ F2, ISO 200.

ACKNOWLEDGEMENTS

My family, Jude, Sean and Emma who love and support me, often from afar. Thank you for being there when I get home at the end of another month away, tired, grumpy and often run-down.

The great athletes of the pro peloton, I am in constant awe of your achievements, please continue to strive for a clean sport so my children can aspire to your heights.

France, I've had a love/hate relationship with France all my life, I'm English after all. Continue with *La Grande Boucle* and you will always have a spot in my heart.

Lewis Blackwell would like to thank: Simon O'Hagan for getting him into road cycling and its disorders; Graham Bence for letting him be first up a hill, once; IG Markets for hospitality and access to the Tour; Rapha and its performance clothes that can make life better looking if no less painful; and Jan and Caledonia for putting up with too much talk about cycling.

The publisher is grateful for literary permission to reproduce items subject to copyright. Every effort has been made to trace the copyright holders and the publisher apologises for any unintentional omissions. We would be pleased to hear from any not acknowledged here and undertake to make all reasonable efforts to include the appropriate acknowledgment in any subsequent editions.

ISBN: 978-174-270353-4
Produced and originated by PQ Blackwell Limited
116 Symonds Street, Auckland, New Zealand
www.pqblackwell.com
Publisher: Geoff Blackwell
Editor-in-Chief: Ruth Hobday

Published in 2012 by Hardie Grant Books
Hardie Grant Books (Australia)
Ground Floor, Building 1
658 Church Street
Richmond, Victoria 3121
www.hardiegrant.com.au

Hardie Grant Books (UK)
Dudley House, North Suite
34–35 Southampton Street
London WC2E 7HF
www.hardiegrant.co.uk

Book Design: Ph.D, A Design Office. www.phdla.com
Image postproduction by danklife.com

Printed by 1010 Printing International Limited, China